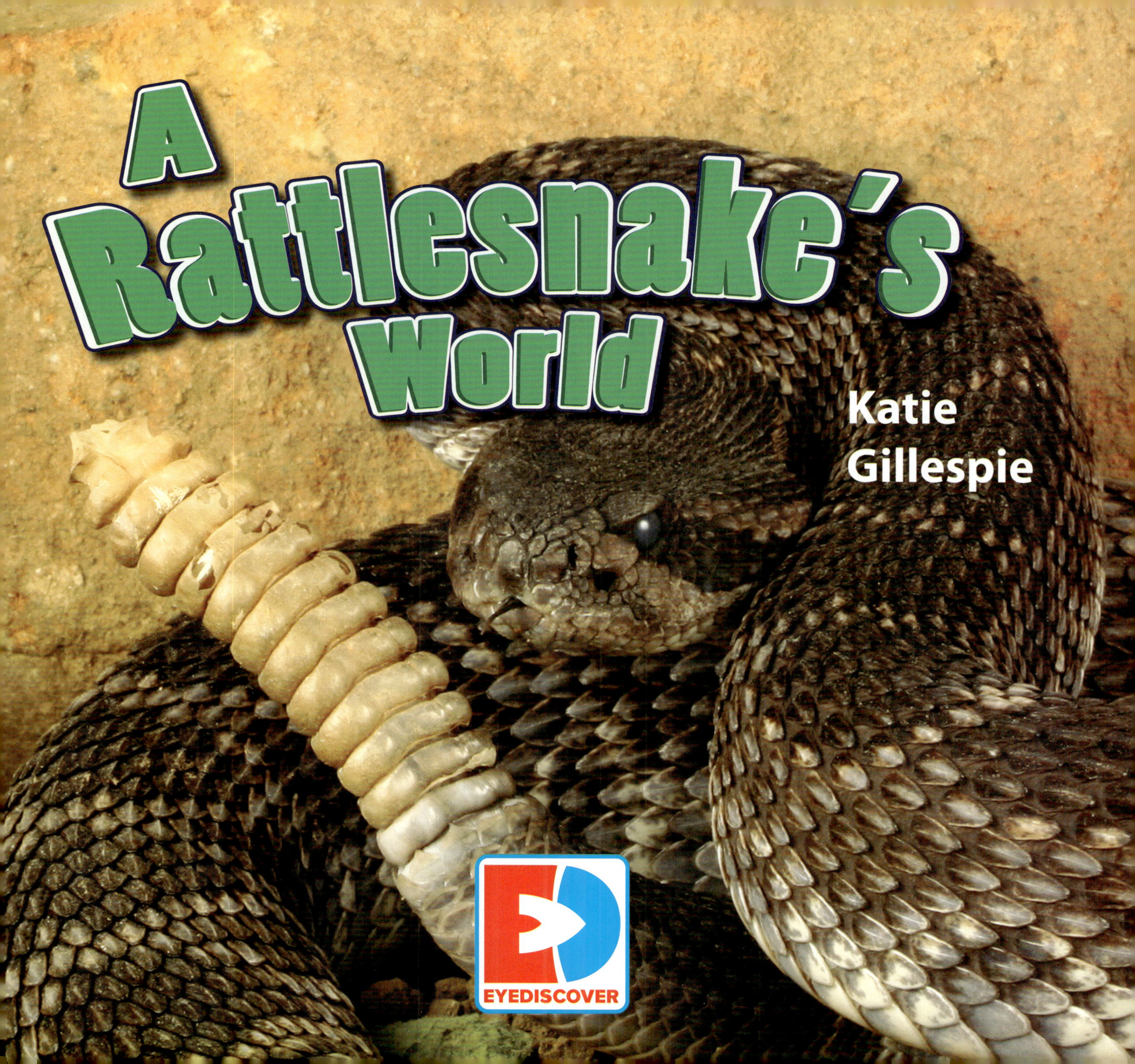
A Rattlesnake's World
Katie Gillespie
EYEDISCOVER

Go to www.eyediscover.com and enter this book's unique code.

BOOK CODE

P954483

EYEDISCOVER brings you optic readalongs that support active learning.

EYEDISCOVER provides enriched content, optimized for tablet use, that supplements and complements this book. EYEDISCOVER books strive to create inspired learning and engage young minds in a total learning experience.

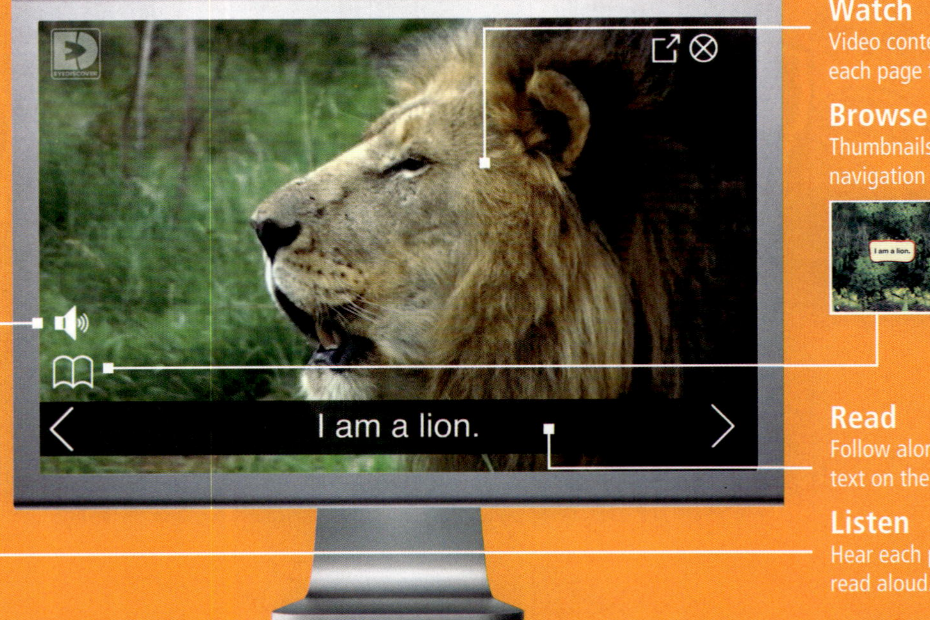

Watch
Video content brings each page to life.

Browse
Thumbnails make navigation simple.

Read
Follow along with text on the screen.

Listen
Hear each page read aloud.

Your EYEDISCOVER Optic Readalongs come alive with...

Audio
Listen to the entire book read aloud.

Video
High resolution videos turn each spread into an optic readalong.

OPTIMIZED FOR
- TABLETS
- WHITEBOARDS
- COMPUTERS
- AND MUCH MORE!

Published by AV^2 by Weigl
350 5th Avenue, 59th Floor New York, NY 10118
Website: www.eyediscover.com

Library of Congress Control Number: 2017930725

ISBN 978-1-4896-5686-5 (hardcover)

Printed in the United States of America
in Brainerd, Minnesota
1 2 3 4 5 6 7 8 9 0 21 20 19 18 17

022017
020317

Editor: Katie Gillespie
Designer: Mandy Christiansen

Weigl acknowledges Getty Images, iStock, Alamy, and Shutterstock as the primary image suppliers for this title.

A Rattlesnake's World

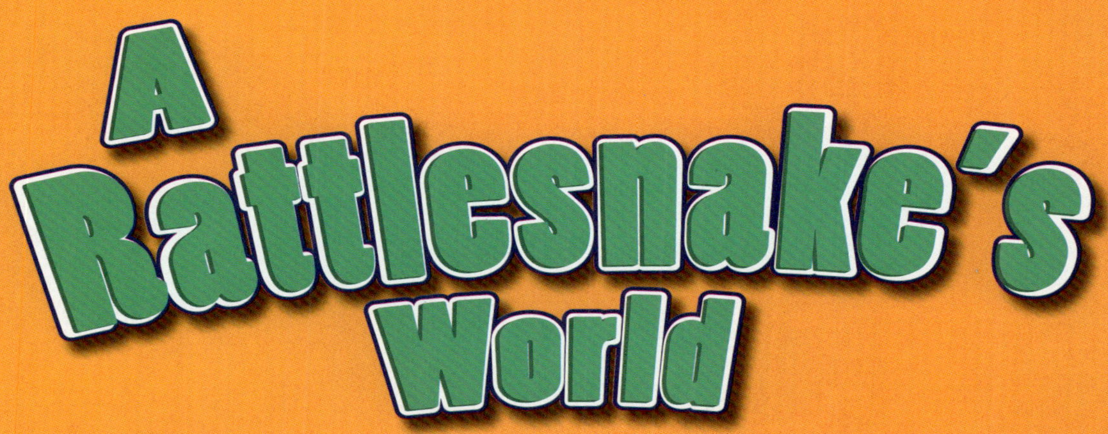

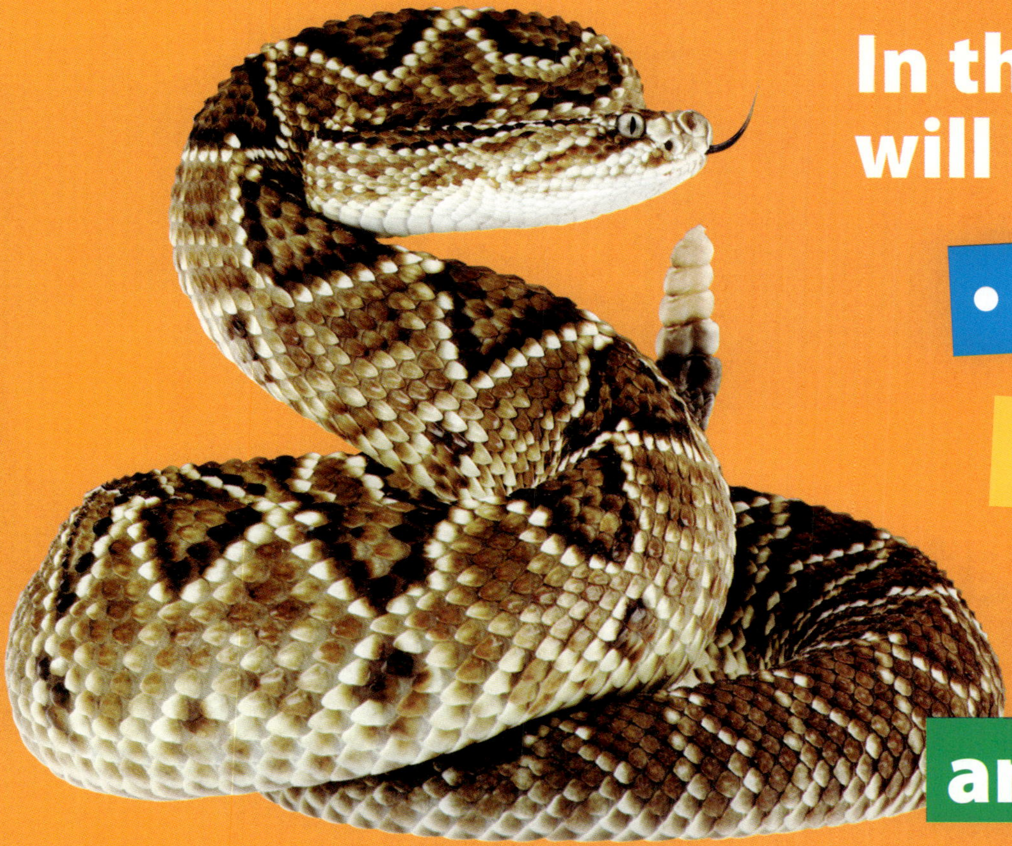

In this book, you will learn about

- how I look
- where I live
- what I eat

and much more!

I am a rattlesnake.

I am a large snake with a rattle on the end of my tail. I am part of the reptile family.

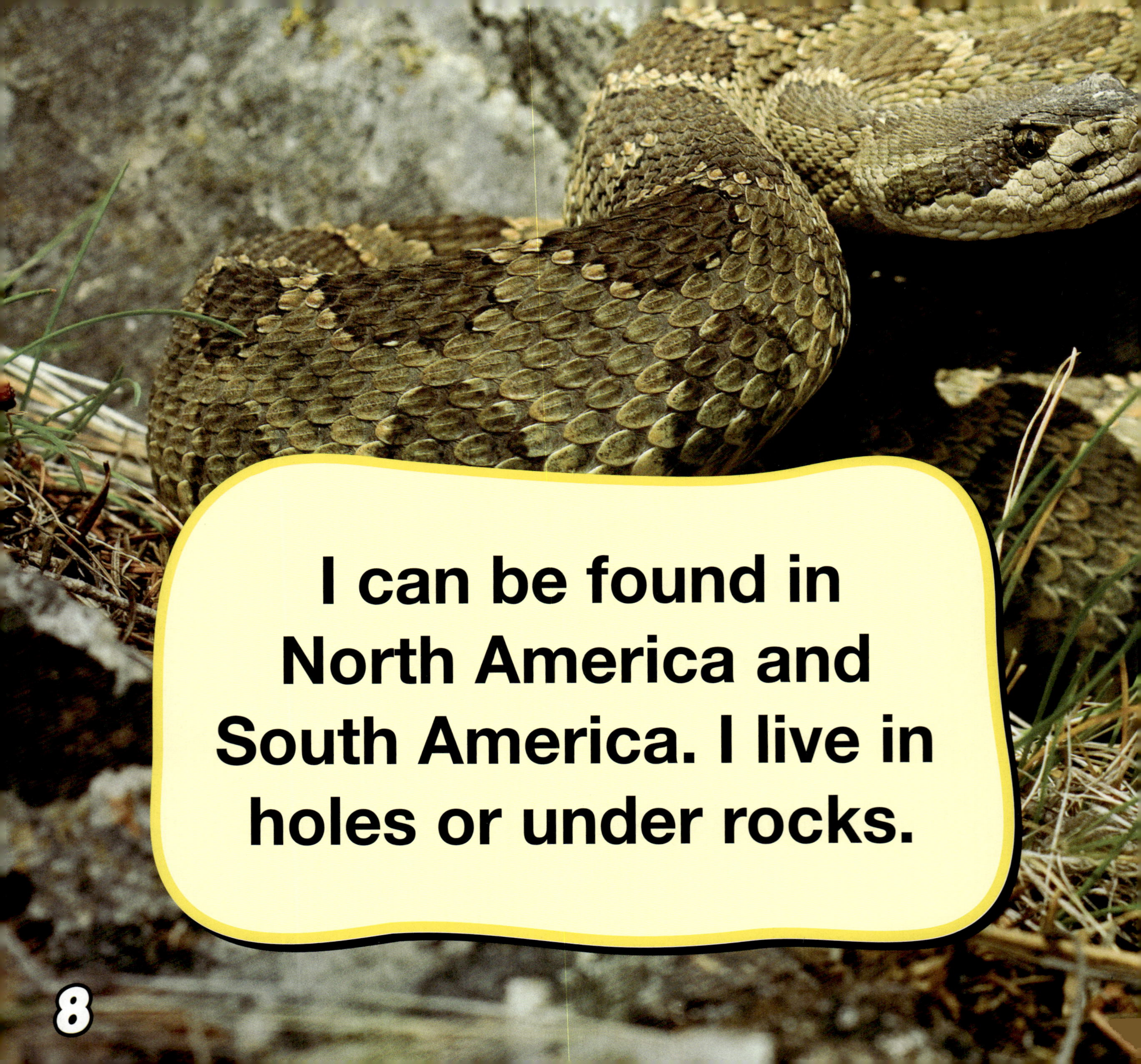

I can be found in North America and South America. I live in holes or under rocks.

I shed my skin three or four times each year. This is called molting.

My rattle gets bigger every time I molt. I shake it when danger is near.

I am a meat eater.
I hunt lizards and
rodents for food.

I have venom to help me hunt. It comes out when I bite.

My tongue is pointed like a fork. I can use my tongue to smell.

I need a safe place to hide when it gets too hot or too cold. This helps me stay healthy and happy.

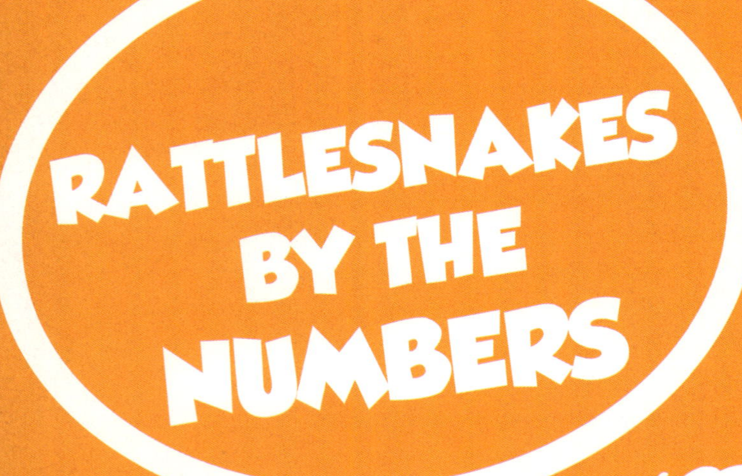

RATTLESNAKES BY THE NUMBERS

It **only** takes **0.5 seconds** for a rattlesnake to **inject** its **prey** with **venom**.

Hundreds of rattlesnakes may share **one** den.

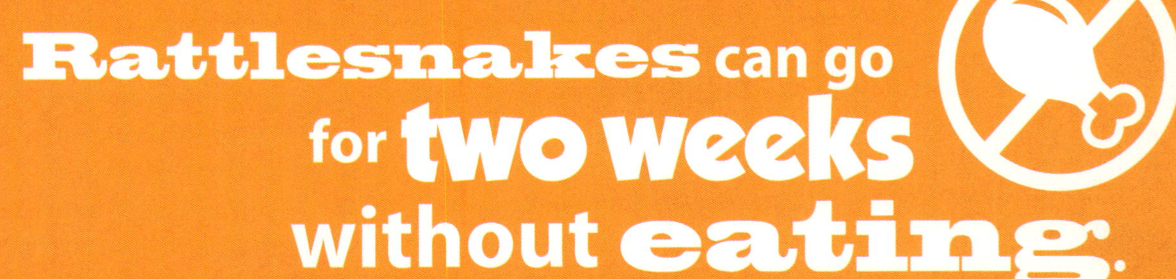

Rattlesnakes can go for **two weeks** without **eating**.

The **largest** rattlesnakes are up to **8 feet long**. (2.4 meters)

A rattlesnake's **rattle** does not make **noise** until it has **two to three rings**.

Female rattlesnakes have babies once every **two years**.

KEY WORDS

Research has shown that as much as 65 percent of all written material published in English is made up of 300 words. These 300 words cannot be taught using pictures or learned by sounding them out. They must be recognized by sight. This book contains 45 common sight words to help young readers improve their reading fluency and comprehension. This book also teaches young readers several important content words, such as proper nouns. These words are paired with pictures to aid in learning and improve understanding.

Page	Sight Words First Appearance
4	a, am, I
7	end, family, large, my, of, on, part, the, with
8	and, be, can, found, in, live, or, under
11	each, four, is, this, three, times, year
12	every, gets, it, near, when
15	food, for
16	comes, have, help, me, out, to
18	like, use
20	need, place, too

Page	Content Words First Appearance
4	rattlesnake
7	rattle, reptile, snake, tail
8	holes, North America, rocks, South America
11	molting, skin
12	danger
15	lizards, meat eater, rodents
16	venom
18	fork, tongue

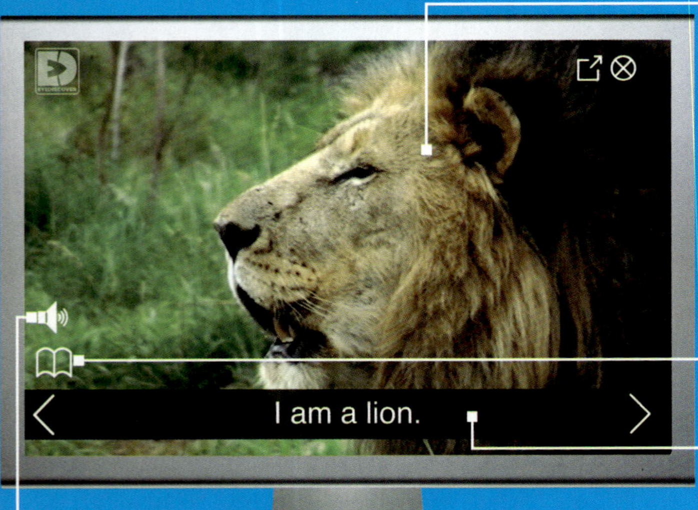

Watch
Video content brings each page to life.

Browse
Thumbnails make navigation simple.

Read
Follow along with text on the screen.

Listen
Hear each page read aloud.

Go to www.eyediscover.com and enter this book's unique code.

BOOK CODE

P954483